SUPER SANDCASTLE
Going Green

WHAT IN THE WORLD IS GREEN ENERGY?

Oona Gaarder-Juntti

Consulting Editor, Diane Craig, M.A./Reading Specialist

ABDO
Publishing Company

Published by ABDO Publishing Company, 8000 West 78th Street, Edina, Minnesota 55439. Copyright © 2011 by Abdo Consulting Group, Inc. International copyrights reserved in all countries. No part of this book may be reproduced in any form without written permission from the publisher. Super SandCastle™ is a trademark and logo of ABDO Publishing Company.

Printed in the United States of America, North Mankato, Minnesota
052010
092010

 PRINTED ON RECYCLED PAPER

Editor: Katherine Hengel
Content Developer: Nancy Tuminelly
Cover and Interior Design and Production: Oona Gaarder-Juntti, Mighty Media
Photo Credits: AbleStock, Shutterstock

Library of Congress Cataloging-in-Publication Data

Gaarder-Juntti, Oona, 1979-
   What in the world is green energy? / Oona Gaarder-Juntti.
      p. cm. -- (Going green)
   ISBN 978-1-61613-191-3
   1. Renewable energy resources--Juvenile literature. I. Title.
   TJ802.2.G33 2011
   333.79--dc22
                                     2010004320

Super SandCastle™ books are created by a team of professional educators, reading specialists, and content developers around five essential components—phonemic awareness, phonics, vocabulary, text comprehension, and fluency—to assist young readers as they develop reading skills and strategies and increase their general knowledge. All books are written, reviewed, and leveled for guided reading, early reading intervention, and Accelerated Reader® programs for use in shared, guided, and independent reading and writing activities to support a balanced approach to literacy instruction.

ABOUT SUPER SANDCASTLE™
Bigger Books for Emerging Readers
Grades K–4

Created for library, classroom, and at-home use, Super SandCastle™ books support and engage young readers as they develop and build literacy skills and will increase their general knowledge about the world around them. Super SandCastle™ books are an extension of SandCastle™, the leading preK–3 imprint for emerging and beginning readers. Super SandCastle™ features a larger trim size for more reading fun.

Let Us Know
Super SandCastle™ would like to hear your stories about reading this book. What was your favorite page? Was there something hard that you needed help with? Share the ups and downs of learning to read. We want to hear from you! Send us an e-mail.

sandcastle@abdopublishing.com

Contact us for a complete list of SandCastle™, Super SandCastle™, and other nonfiction and fiction titles from ABDO Publishing Company.

www.abdopublishing.com • 8000 West 78th Street Edina, MN 55439 • 800-800-1312 • 952-831-1632 fax

Contents

WHAT IN THE WORLD IS BEING GREEN?

Being green means taking care of the earth. Many things on our planet are connected. When one thing changes, it can cause something else to change. That's why the way we treat the earth is so important. Keeping the earth healthy can seem like a big job. You can help by saving energy and **resources** every day.

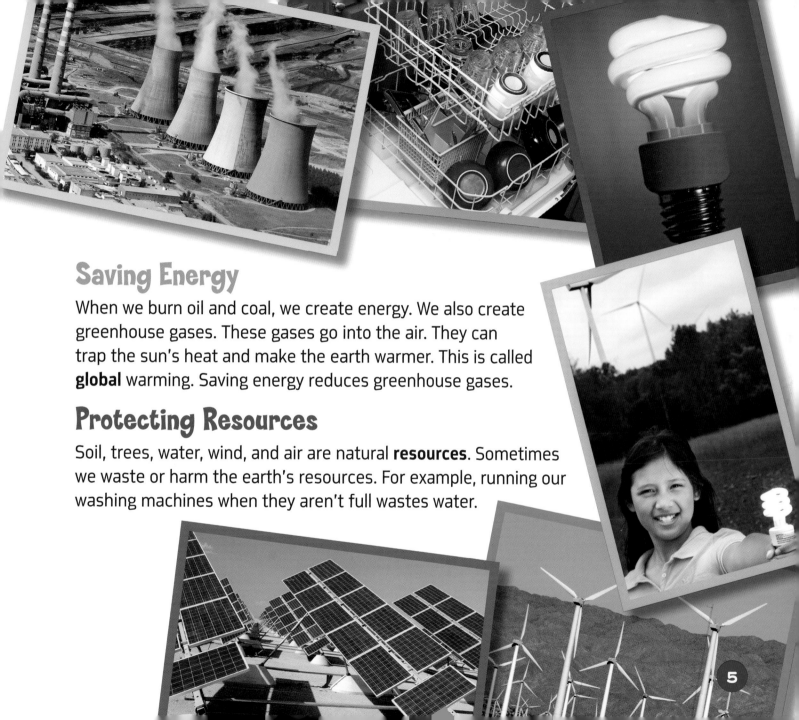

Saving Energy

When we burn oil and coal, we create energy. We also create greenhouse gases. These gases go into the air. They can trap the sun's heat and make the earth warmer. This is called **global** warming. Saving energy reduces greenhouse gases.

Protecting Resources

Soil, trees, water, wind, and air are natural **resources**. Sometimes we waste or harm the earth's resources. For example, running our washing machines when they aren't full wastes water.

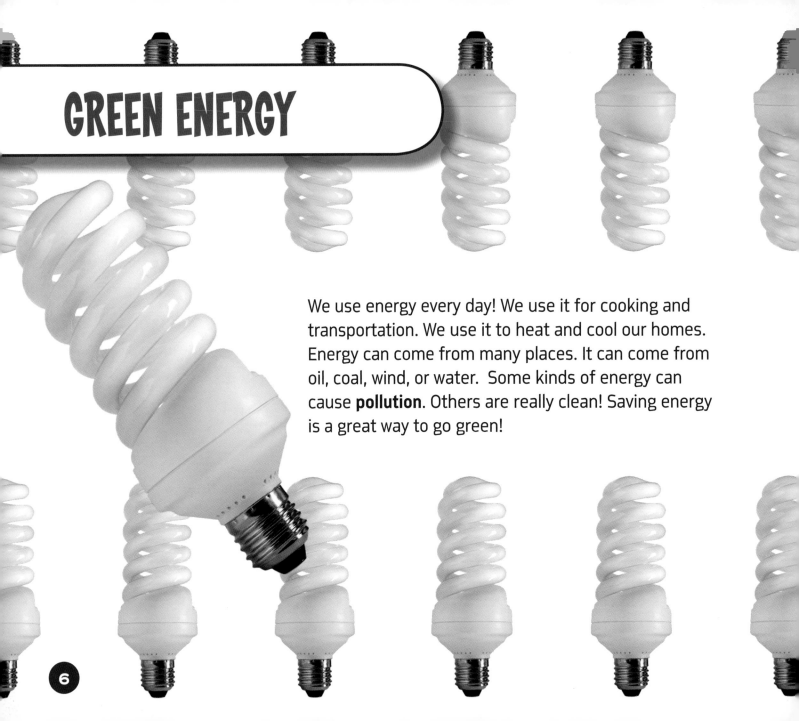

GREEN ENERGY

We use energy every day! We use it for cooking and transportation. We use it to heat and cool our homes. Energy can come from many places. It can come from oil, coal, wind, or water. Some kinds of energy can cause **pollution**. Others are really clean! Saving energy is a great way to go green!

In 2006, wind turbines made enough electricity for 2.4 million homes!

The United States uses 25 percent of the world's energy **resources**.

Waterpower has been used to **grind** grain for more than 2,000 years.

IN A GREEN WORLD

There are many different ways that we use energy every day. How do you use energy?

9

IN A GREEN WORLD

Saving energy helps the earth. Here are some ways to use less energy every day.

Use a microwave oven to heat up small amounts of food.

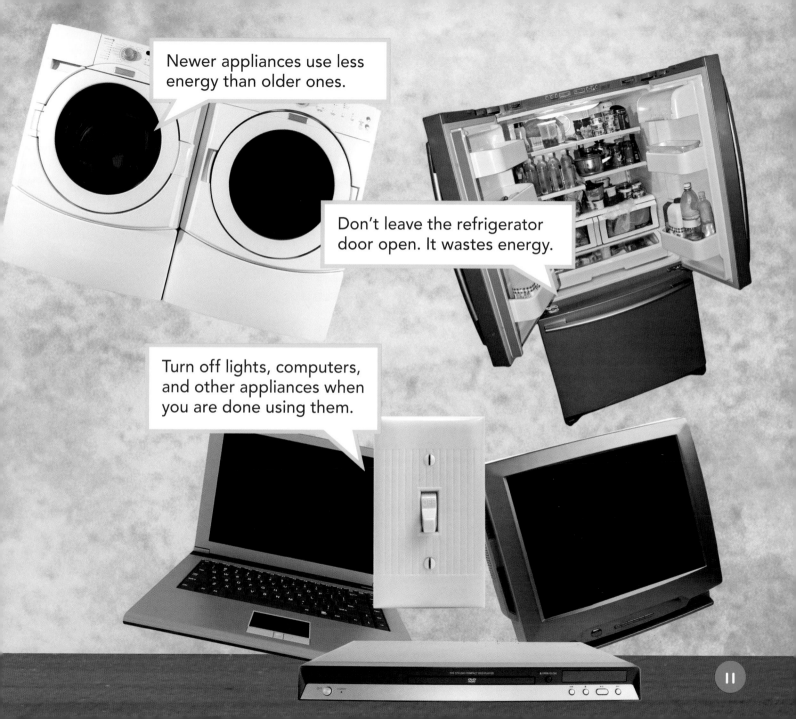

IN A GREEN WORLD

Using energy sources that won't run out is good for the earth.

A hybrid car uses both gas and electricity.

Fuel for cars can be made from corn and other plants.

The wind spins big machines to make electricity.

Solar panels turn the sun's rays into electricity.

13

HOW YOU CAN HELP

Everyone knows the 3 Rs. Reduce, Reuse, and Recycle. Do you know how to practice the 3 Rs with energy? The next few pages will show you how. Think about how you use energy and where it comes from. There are many ways to save energy!

Saving is Easy

It pays to save electrical energy. Really! You can help the earth and your family. One way is to use compact **fluorescent** lightbulbs (CFLs). They use less energy than other bulbs. That means less electricity! You can also unplug electronics. They use energy even when they aren't turned on!

CFLs last ten times longer than other bulbs.

Learn about Resources

Energy comes from **resources**. Some resources are nonrenewable. Others are renewable.

Nonrenewable resources cannot be replaced quickly. We could run out of them. Oil, gas, and coal are nonrenewable resources. And when we burn them for energy, we cause **pollution**.

Renewable **resources** are different. Wind, water, plants, and the sun are renewable resources. We won't run out of them! Learn more about renewable resources on the next pages.

Clean Energy to the Rescue!

There are many kinds of renewable **resources**. They can create clean energy! Here are some that we can use.

Wind

The wind spins big machines called wind turbines to make electricity.

Sun

The sun's rays can be turned into energy! **Solar panels** turn the rays into electricity. Three scientists at AT&T Bell Laboratories made the first solar panel in 1954.

Water

Running water is very powerful. It can be used to make electricity.

Plants

Energy can be made from corn and other plants. We can use it to make fuel for cars.

Earth

The middle of the earth is very hot. We can drill into it for energy!

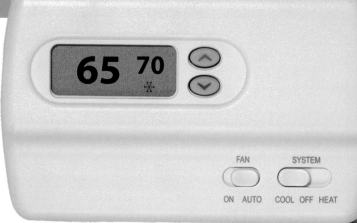

Turn it Down

Homes use a lot of energy. You can **adjust** your **thermostat** to save energy. Turn down the heat or air conditioner when you won't be home. Ask your parents about your thermostat. Many thermostats can be set to change the temperature automatically.

Open the curtains in the winter to let in sunlight. Close the curtains in the summer to keep the room cool.

Run it Full

Run your dishwasher and washing machine only when they are full. You can save up to 1,000 gallons (3,785 L) of water a month! Washing clothes in cold water saves energy. Hang your clothes on a line to dry when you can.

LET'S THINK GREEN

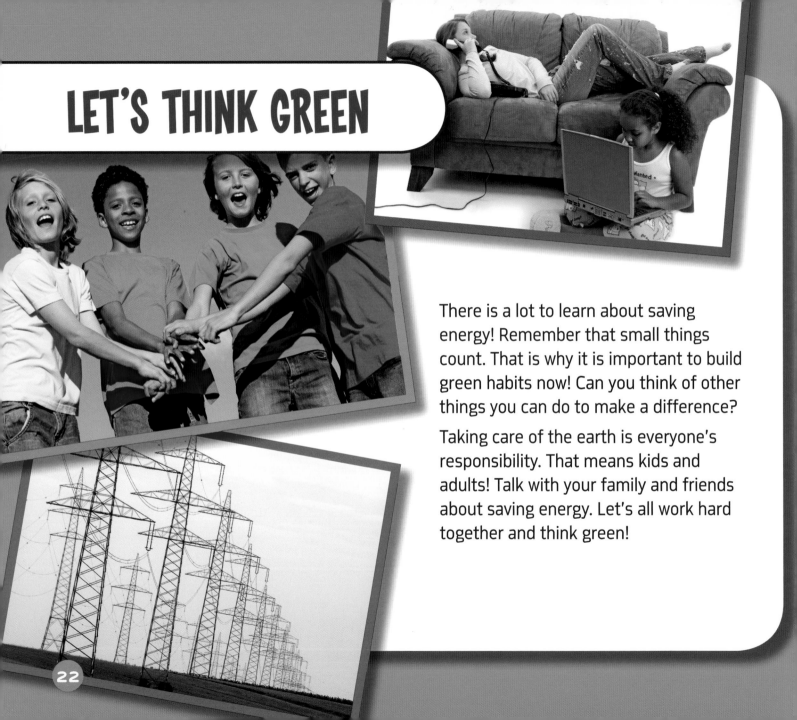

There is a lot to learn about saving energy! Remember that small things count. That is why it is important to build green habits now! Can you think of other things you can do to make a difference?

Taking care of the earth is everyone's responsibility. That means kids and adults! Talk with your family and friends about saving energy. Let's all work hard together and think green!

TAKE THE GREEN PLEDGE

I promise to help the earth every day by doing things in a different way.

I can save energy by:

♻ Using CFLs instead of other lightbulbs.

♻ Unplugging my electronics when I am not using them.

♻ Using natural light whenever I can.

♻ Running the dishwasher only when it is full.

GLOSSARY

adjust – to change something slightly.

fluorescent – giving out a bright light, such as ultraviolet light.

global – having to do with the whole earth.

grind – to crush something into a powder.

pollution – contamination of the air, water, or soil caused by man-made waste.

resource – the supply or source of something. A *natural resource* is a resource found in nature, such as water or trees.

solar panel – a device that turns the sun's light into energy.

thermostat – a device that senses temperature changes and controls heating and cooling systems.